The Gift of Crystals

Connect to the power of soul-healing crystals

RACHELLE CHARMAN

ROCKPOOL
PUBLISHING

A Rockpool Book
PO Box 252
Summer Hill NSW 2130
Australia
www.rockpoolpublishing.com.au
www.facebook.com/RockpoolPublishing

First published in 2012 by Rockpool Publishing as
Crystals ISBN 978-1-921878-70-1.
This edition published in 2019
A catalogue in publication for this book is available from the
National Library of Australia.

ISBN 978-1-925017-82-3

Cover design by Trenett Ha, Rockpool Publishing
Internal design and typesetting by Tracy Loughlin, Rockpool
Publishing
Illustrations by Shutterstock

Images: Tiger's Eye: **Weinrich Minerals, Inc, www.weinrich-mineralsinc.com**; Spirit Quartz: **www.heartoftheearth.com.au**;
Ajoite, Amazonite, Apatite — Green, Aquamarine, Aragonite,
Azurite, Bixbite, Brazilianite, Bustamite, Calcite, Chrysocolla,
Danburite, Diamond, Diopside, Dioptase, Emerald, Kunzite,
Morganite, Phenacite, Purpurite, Pyrite, Tanzanite, Topaz,
Tourmaline — Blue, Green, Pink and Red: **Rob Lavinsky, www.mineralatlas.com**; Black Obsidian, Aventurine, Agate, Amber,
Amethyst, Ametrine, Andalusite — Chiastolite, Angelite,
Apache Tears, Apophyllite, Barnacle, Tourmaline — Black
and Brown, Bloodstone, Boji Stones™, Blue Lace Agate,
Cacoxenite, Cathedral Lightbrary, Celestite, Channelling
Dow, Chrysoprase, Citrine, Crocoite, Devic Temple, Double

Terminator, Dumortierite, Elestial, Eudialyte, Fluorite, Fulgurite,
Galena, Golden Calcite, Grounding Crystal, Helidor, Herkimer,
Hiddenite, Isis, Jade, Jasper — Mookite, Ocean and Red, Jet,
Key, Labradorite, Lapis Lazuli, Larimar, Laser Wand, Lemurian
Seeded, Libyan Gold Tektite, Manifestation Crystal, Moldavite,
Moonstone, Nirvana Quartz, Nuummite, Orpiment, Pietersite,
Phantom, Prehnite, Pyromorphite, Quartz, Rainbow Crystal, Record
Keeper, Rhodonite, Rose Quartz, Ruby, Scolecite, Selenite,
Self Healed, Seraphinite, Serpentine, Shaman Stone, Shattuckite,
Shiva Lingam, Sodalite, Smoky Quartz, Spirit Quartz, Sungite,
Sunstone, Surgilite, Tabby, Tantric Twin, Tektite, Tibetan
Quartz, Tiger Eye, Time Link, Transmitter, Turquoise, Vivianite,
Window, Zincite, Fairy Stone, Tree Root, Malachite and Azurite,
Malachite and Chrysocolla: **Matt Walker, www. facebook.com/MattWalkerImages**; Apatite — Blue, Carnelian, Charoite,
Chrysanthemum Stone, Chrysoberyl, Cinnabar, Crocoite, Cuprite,
Fire Agate, Garnet, Goethite, Hematite, Kyanite — Blue,
Lepidolite, Malachite, Natrolite, Opal, Peridot, Petrified Wood,
Rodochrosite, Rutilated Quartz, Stibnite, Watermelon Tourmaline:
John H. Betts, www. johnbetts-fineminerals.com
Additional images by Nebula Design Studios

Thank you to The Wizard of Auz for the use of some images supplied
with Matt Walker. The Wizard of Auz sources and trades
globally. They are especially known for their extensive range of
rare and unusual crystals and gemstones, which they supply as
natural forms, carvings and shapes, or beads and trinkets.
They are members of the Fair Trade Association of Australia and
New Zealand and are very conscientious about product sourcing
and ethics; **www.wizardofauz.com**, **www.facebook.com/wizauz**,
Twitter @WizardofAuz. In Australia 1-800 THE WIZARD.

Printed in China
10 9 8 7 6 5 4 3 2 1

Contents

INTRODUCTION

This book is a gift to you, the reader, from my heart to assist you on your deep journey of transformation and awakening as you connect to and explore the Crystal Kingdom and its magic. The information in this book will guide and encourage you to have your own experiences with the Crystal Kingdom as you bring through your own wisdom and knowledge of this powerful medicine from the Earth.

The intention for this book is for you to empower yourself on your journey through life. All of us are searching in some way for a tool that can assist us in moving through our challenges into a place of empowerment and joy in our lives. We sometimes search outside ourselves looking for the answers. I truly believe everything we need to know lies within each and every one of us, now and always. The beauty of crystals is they inspire us to delve deep within ourselves as we connect to our own internal wisdom and knowledge. Please take what feels right within the pages of this book and leave what doesn't and, more importantly, find your own way and your own connection to your heart and divine mission here on Earth.

As you read through this book, you will be guided and supported to journey deep within the Crystal Kingdom and its medicine of love. On this journey you will unlock and bring forth your own wisdom and knowledge, awakening to your own divine truth. Creating your own unique connection with the Crystal Kingdom is essential and, I believe, very important part of your own healing process. Owning and listening to your own inner wisdom is important for truly stepping into your power.

We can invite crystals into our lives in various different ways. Having these beautiful crystals in the home creates an environment for transformation. You can sit quietly with your crystal, simply setting your intention to tune into its healing energy. You will also benefit from a crystal's healing properties simply by holding, wearing, or having a crystal in your pocket because your energy field will start to mirror the energy field of the crystal's pure structure, bringing balance and healing.

I truly believe crystals are gifts from Mother Earth, to support us on our divine journey back to love. As we connect and work with crystals we create divine union with and reconnection to our Mother Earth and our source, experiencing oneness and joy.

Please know and remember my heart is with you as you embark on this sacred journey into the Crystal Kingdom.

Crystals

Crystals are divine gifts and sacred tools from Mother Earth that assist us in our growth, transformation and healing. They are one of the many medicines of the planet, with each crystal holding a specific energy that can assist us in our healing process. The Earth's core is made up of 85 per cent crystal, so in reality we are living on one big ball of crystal.

Crystals are definitely more than just pretty rocks; they're alive and have a consciousness of their own. I believe that all crystals hold unique, loving energies that assist humanity in discovering our true divine magnificence. As we connect to a crystal and its energy, it allows us to align and connect to the same healing energy that exists within each of us. Crystals radiate Divine Love and pure energy from Mother Earth and the universe, and amplify and reflect back to us the beauty within our hearts, allowing us the opportunity to heal ourselves. In this process, our emotional, mental, spiritual and physical bodies can attain balance. Crystals encourage and assist us to live in the now so we start to truly understand that we are all connected to the universe at all times. Crystals remind us of our true essence of oneness and connection to source.

So you can get a deeper understanding of how this works, I would like to share with you a little information about the science of crystals and our sacred connection to them. Everything in this universe is made up of energy and vibration. The science that explains this is Sacred Geometry, which is an in-depth study of how everything in the universe is connected to the one source — universal energy. There are five main shapes, or blueprints, that energy organises and aligns itself to as it manifests into the physical form. All life on the planet stems from these shapes, called the five platonic solids.

Crystals are pure energy made up of atoms. These atoms are the inner structure of energy. Crystals are formed and birthed when these atoms of energy align to different forms, the platonic solids. This process allows each crystal to be unique, each holding a different energy, colour and vibration. Everything on this physical plane is created from these energetic structures, all vibrating at different frequencies with different combinations of these atoms aligning through the five platonic solids and Sacred Geometry. This tells us that everything is connected to the same universal source at our core.

The sacred relationship that's created between us and the Crystal Kingdom allows for deep transformation and healing to occur on many levels. Crystals hold within them the secrets to healing as they assist humanity in our journey back to peace and wellbeing. The healing energy of the crystals merges with the body's energy fields, promoting harmony and balance. The similarities between crystals and the human body allow the cells of the body to communicate with each other, creating a transfer of energy and allowing the innate intelligence of the body to heal itself. Crystal healing is actually a science and works within a law of physics, the law of resonance, which states 'like energy attracts like energy'. This is why, when we are in the presence of crystals, they assist us in aligning with the same healing energy that is within.

Through our lives we experience many challenges that we sometimes misinterpret, which then creates much pain, hurt and fear, and we tend to shut off from ourselves and those around us. This process can start to create suppressed emotions within our energy field that can lay dormant, creating unwanted behavioural patterns in our lives. This imbalance in our energy body can eventually create disease within the physical body. These suppressed emotions, old patterns and belief systems are stored in our energy fields and become our emotional baggage. This can then create the feeling that we are not whole. The illusion of separation from our source starts to take place as we begin to identify ourselves as our issues instead of our true essence and divinity.

Crystals create a sacred, safe space for us to discard these old, suppressed emotions and unwanted patterns from our fields. Crystals know they are pure love and light of the universe. They gently assist us in connecting our higher selves with our pure essence as we align to the love and order of the universe, allowing transformation and deep healing to occur. The crystal vibration resonates with the energy in the body and the auric field, and the imbalance rises as a memory of the past. As we are held in the vibration of love and truth and with our hearts open, we are able to expand our awareness to see the truth within these experiences, and are given an opportunity to accept and release the issue. We move out of the old way of being and receive the blessings and gifts from such an experience. We surrender and set ourselves free from the chains of our old perception as we move deeper into our hearts and accept, love and nurture more aspects of ourselves. This process creates a deep connection between our heart and soul, and an opportunity to look deeply into the inner self with unconditional love and trust.

From my own experience of healing I have come to understand that our most powerful gifts are hidden beneath our fears in those places that we feel uncomfortable in. Some call this place the shadow. I believe that this is where our power lies and our true gifts are revealed. There is always a blessing with a painful challenge — we just have to have the courage to look for it. This is a sacred process of healing and, when truly understood and felt in the heart, it allows us much growth and an expanded awareness of ourselves that creates deep transformation and awakening. It creates much gratitude for life and allows us to know and accept ourselves completely. This healing journey makes us who we are, and creates great strength and courage of spirit.

Crystals and the past

Numerous cultures throughout history have harnessed the powerful energies of crystals. As far back as Atlantis, crystals have been respected, understood and recognised as energetic templates of divine knowledge and wisdom. The Atlanteans were from an advanced civilisation that used crystals in various forms for healing, gaining universal knowledge and spiritual awakening. They understood the forces that are generated by crystals and worked within these energetic laws to benefit their people.

In Australia, the Aboriginal peoples would connect to certain crystals to assist in entering the Dreamtime.

Native Americans also understood crystals and their vast range of magical properties. They viewed them as among their most sacred possessions. Native Americans used the energetic properties of Quartz crystals to amplify and strengthen their own healing abilities and their connection to Mother Earth.

In preparation for entering into spiritual initiations the ancient Egyptians would grind crystals such as Lapis Lazuli and Carnelian to wear as makeup to assist in this process. Crystals have been found entombed with Egyptian mummies as part of the customary practice that assisted the dead to travel safely into the afterlife.

In South America, Peru and Mexico, several crystal skulls have been discovered. The most famous of these is the Mitchell-Hedges skull, which was found in the Mayan temples in Mexico. It is believed the skull assists humanity in our collective awakening and our journey into oneness.

Crystals and the modern world

It is very exciting that modern-day sciences are beginning to understand the vast properties of crystals and their energy, and how we can utilise these powerful properties. Crystals play a huge role in our lives and are utilised in various ways. Crystals are found in many different machines that run our technology. They are used in computers to hold the memory, are found in our watches to keep the time and are even found in our television sets. The techno world would not exist today if it was not for the Crystal Kingdom because most of our modern technology is run on crystal energy in some form or another. Crystals are being increasingly used for their healing purposes in modern medicine. Silicon crystal chips are used in pacemakers and rubies are used in surgical lasers. Crystals are also used in natural medicines by extracting the healing energies from the crystal and dissolving them in water for use as a base for medicines called gem essences or elixirs.

Cleansing and energising crystals

It is essential to cleanse and energise your crystals on a regular basis for several reasons. Science has proven that crystals store and retain energy so it is important that you clear the energy from them to keep your crystals clear and vibrant. Crystals come from deep within the Earth and when we remove them from their natural environment they lose their potent energy, so we are required to charge them back to their natural state.

Cleansing re-energises the crystal and ensures it is functioning at its full potential, clearing any previous energies such as other people's thoughts and emotions. You will intuitively know when it is time to cleanse your crystals because they may look and feel dull in energy, or you may even pick up other energies radiating from the crystals.

Crystals amplify the light within. The more love you share with them, the more love and light they radiate back to you. I personally recommend you cleanse and charge your crystals at least once a month. Cleansing and charging your crystals before and after each healing is very important.

Cleansing methods

Following are some of the many ways and processes used to charge and cleanse crystals. Remember, there is no right or wrong way to cleanse and charge your crystals. Make sure to tune in to and work with the process that feels most effective for you. The most important aspect of this process is to set a strong intention of cleansing, then apply your specific cleansing technique.

Water

Certain crystals are sensitive to water, usually those with striations or with soft or brittle textures. Use other methods to cleanse and charge these crystals.

Salt water — Crystals love a visit to the beach. Dip your crystals into the sea. Be sure to rinse them with fresh water afterwards and dry them with a cloth. The salt assists in dissolving any unwanted energies.

Fresh water — When cleansing crystals with fresh water, choose water that is energetically clear, such as rain water or water in nature. If you are unable to find these water sources, use bottled or distilled water. If you choose tap water, clear the water energetically with Reiki, clearing pendants or pure intention before you use it.

Natural springs, waterfalls and streams — Place your crystals in nature to assist in their rejuvenation.

Sound

Crystals enjoy a sound bath because it brings the crystal back to its natural vibration. It turns the crystal on and amplifies its energy.

Voice — Hold the intention of cleansing your crystal and allow yourself to move into a space of clarity. Tone directly into your crystal, giving the sound the freedom to emanate whatever tone manifests. This method will powerfully align your energy with the vibration of the crystal.

Tuning forks, Tibetan bells and bowls, and crystal bowls — Sound the instrument while moving it over the crystal with the intention of clearing and energising the crystal.

Music — Soft, high vibrational and spiritual music playing in a room will cleanse and energise your crystals.

Other cleansing techniques

Smudging — The most effective herbs or incense for smudging are sage and frankincense. Burn in a bowl, creating cleansing smoke, and set the intention of cleansing as you blow the smoke over the crystals.

Visualisation — Create a simple visualisation of a waterfall and see your crystals being cleansed under the crystal clear water.

Light — Visualise and invoke golden or violet light and see this light penetrate into your crystal, setting the intention of cleansing.

Reiki — Crystals love Reiki energy. You can cleanse and charge your crystals by placing a clearing or charging symbol into them.

Energising methods

Many methods can be used to energise or charge your crystals.

Sunlight — The sun will charge your crystal with masculine energy qualities such as strength, power and assertiveness. Crystals originate from Mother Earth and usually don't like a lot of direct sunlight. Too much sunlight can discolour your crystals and heat changes the chemical structure. Charge your crystals in direct sunlight for no more than a few hours.

Moonlight — Crystals love a beautiful moon bath. Just like us, crystals are affected strongly by the phases of the moon due to the water element that exists within us and crystals. You can place your crystal under any phase of the moon, with the full moon being the most potent. The magnetic charge and pull on the Earth during this time assists in energising the crystal. It is best to lay the crystals on the Earth under the moon. However, if you live in a place where this is not possible, you can still energise your crystals by moonlight by placing them in a pot plant next to a window or on a balcony under direct moonlight. The moon will charge your crystals with feminine energies such as compassion, healing and nurturing.

Energy grids — Energy grids are vortexes of light where the energy is high, pure and constantly charging. You can create your own grid, or work with copper pyramids. Place the crystals within the grid, where they will be charged with universal energy.

Mother Earth — Crystals originally come from the Earth. Placing your crystal back into the Earth will fully restore its natural energy and beauty. Make sure to connect with the crystal to find out how long it would like to be left in the Earth. A short part of a day can restore your crystal to its full potential; however, each crystal is unique.

Other crystals — Crystal clusters and geode caves still remain in their natural state and continuously recharge themselves, so they are ideal for recharging other crystals. Place your crystal into a crystal geode cave or onto a crystal cluster.

Energy pendants — Several energy pendants designed to clear and recharge energies are available on the market.

Connecting to your crystals

Crystals invite us all to connect deeply with their essence and energy so they can assist us on our healing journey. Each crystal has a special and unique message, medicine and energy to share with us.

The word 'crystal' comes from the Greek word krustallos, meaning ice or frozen light. Crystals are pure light and energy, and light is a medium of information. Each crystal is a channel of Divine Love and wisdom from the universe and the Earth with knowledge to impart.

Crystals are a divine reflection of our soul and mirror back to us the love that is our pure essence and true state of being. Crystals share the truth of our existence and inner knowing, and assist us in bringing this awareness to the surface for us to receive and believe in ourselves.

Creating the time and space to connect to your crystals individually will bring your understanding of crystals and your own healing journey to a whole new level, allowing you to deepen your understanding of these amazing gifts from the Earth. The following guide will help you in your practice.

Gently close your eyes

Bring your awareness to your breath, the in breath and the out.

Allow yourself to let go and relax.

With each breath you take you become more and more relaxed.

Become aware now of your own heartbeat.

Drop deeply into this loving vibration, dropping deeper and deeper.

Feel yourself journey deep into the heart of the Earth.

Feel your heart begin to merge and beat as one with our divine Earth Mother.

Open and receive the love and healing that is created from this sacred connection.

Now place your crystal on your heart centre, feeling deeply into its heartbeat.

Breathe in this loving healing vibration, as your heart beats as one with this powerful medicine of the Earth.

Now invoke and call upon the spirit and Deva of this beautiful crystal. As the Deva enters into your sacred space, it showers you in this healing light and crystal love.

Open fully to receive this blessing from the Crystal Kingdom.

Allow this crystal energy to flow from your heart into every cell of your being.

Radiate this healing vibration out into your auric field as you connect deeply, becoming one with your crystal.

Work now gently with your breath.

Inhale deeply. On the inhale, your crystal pulsates and radiates its loving, healing energy back into your heart. On the exhale send love from your heart and offer this love into the heart of your crystal.

Breathe like this for a few minutes, sharing this sacred healing space together as this loving being of the Crystal Kingdom assists you in activating and awakening the powerful healing energy that lies within.

Become aware of how you feel and what you are experiencing as you connect deeply to this sacred medicine.

Open now to receive any wisdom or messages this crystal has to share.

Take a moment to thank your crystal for sharing this sacred space and for all the healing you have received. Know that you are one with this loving gift from Mother Earth and there is no separation.

Bring your awareness back into the room.

Call all aspects of your self into the here and now.

Gently open your eyes.

Crystal grids

Creating crystal grids is as simple as laying crystals in a specific pattern to create an energy vortex, amplifying the healing energy of the crystals and your chosen intention. You can place grids in your home, around your garden, in your healing room, on the Earth and around your vision board to amplify the crystals' healing energy for a specific purpose. Crystal grids are a powerful way to use crystal energy to amplify their vast healing properties. Crystals' energy is lessened when they are removed from the Earth and creating grids is a powerful way of amplifying and keeping crystals charged.

The grids create potent energy vortexes that amplify the crystal energy, constantly charging each other and the crystals in the grid. The crystal grid amplifies the energy of the crystal that is placed in the centre, which is called the anchor crystal, creating an amplified energy field around the grid and out into the physical environment.

You can use various formations to create grids. I have come to understand that working with the sacred symbol and structure of the six-pointed star and laying the crystals in this form creates a very powerful and potent grid and vortex. The six-pointed star formation has been used for thousands of years and has the qualities of bringing spirit energy and higher vibrational frequencies into the physical plane. This makes the six-pointed star the perfect formation to use for grid work.

Placing a crystal in the centre, then laying the six-terminated crystals (crystals with a point at the end) in the six-pointed star formation and activating the grid or formation will create your grid and energy vortex. Once the grid is activated it will constantly amplify and charge itself as the anchor crystal builds energy and spreads out from the grid, allowing the healing energy and specific intention of the grid to fill the whole environment in a very powerful and potent way.

Grids can also be programmed by placing and projecting an intention into the grid. The crystals in the grid store the intention and continuously amplify it, making it a powerful manifestation tool. You do not have to program all your grids; you can simply activate the grid to amplify the energies of the anchor crystal and specific grid choice.

Always work with cleansed and charged crystals. Once you activate the grid the energy will continue to amplify until the grid crystals have been moved or knocked. When establishing your grids I suggest you create a sacred space because this is a powerful ritual and the energy you create will manifest into your grid. Make sure to do this when you are feeling centred and calm because the crystals will pick up on your energy and amplify it.

Creating your own crystal grids

In healing rooms — You can place your grid under your healing table, or touching the sides of the wall, so you are actually inside the grid. Choose which healing energy you would like to create and select the crystals that resonate to that frequency. Rose Quartz and Amethyst are great crystals to place within your grids in a healing room because they will fill your sacred space with love and healing energy.

In and around your home — Place grids in different rooms of your home to create and amplify crystal energies. Blue Lace Agate and Blue Calcite are ideal to place in your lounge room because they create clear and peaceful communication. Creating a grid around your home will create an energy of peace and tranquillity.

When charging crystals — Create a grid and program it with the intention of cleansing and charging your crystals, then place your crystals inside the grid.

When programming — You can also program the grid with affirmations, mantras, prayers or specific intentions to assist you in all areas of your life.

When distance healing — Work with healing crystals in the centre of the grid and place a photo or the name of the person you would like to send healing to under the crystal in the centre. Call upon the person's Guides and Angels to send healing energy into the grid and ask that the healing be for their highest good. See the person as already healed, perfect, whole and complete. Ask the higher self of the person to whom you are sending healing to let you know when to take down the grid.

Around vegetable gardens — Plants receive the loving energies of crystals organically. Placing a grid around your garden will assist in the growth and health of your plants and vegetables.

Around vision boards — Placing a grid around your vision board will strengthen the opportunity for you to manifest your dreams and goals.

Around healing centres — Creating a grid buried in the Earth around your healing centre amplifies the energy of the sacred land and the intention of the healing space. This grid assists in keeping your sacred space clean and filled with divine energy of love from the universe.

For space clearing — Setting the intention of clearing energies from a specific space and creating a grid to hold this intention creates a space clearing vortex.

For Earth healing — Create crystal grids on the Earth to assist in the regeneration of our planet. Send mantras and prayers into your grid with the intention of healing the Earth.

Crystals you need to create a grid

Six Clear Quartz terminator points (single or double pointed) are required to create a grid in the shape of a six-pointed star.

Place your chosen crystal in the centre (this is the anchor crystal). This crystal will create the specific energy you would like amplified by your grid.

Use a wand or small Clear Quartz single terminator point to activate the grid. The larger the crystal, the more energy the grid will amplify. When you have activated the six-pointed star grid you can add more crystals to the grid, creating a mandala, in any shape or form. Remain open to becoming a channel for where the crystals would like to lay in the grid. This is a very intuitive process.

Grid activation

Start by creating a sacred space, calling in your Guides and Angels and Devas of the crystals. You may also like to invoke the four elements and directions, Mother Earth and Divine Spirit.

Lay your six Clear Quartz terminated crystals in the shape of a six-pointed star, with the terminations pointing inwards.

Place your desired crystal (anchor crystal) in the centre and place your wand crystal or point in your hand.

Visualise golden light streaming down from the cosmos into your crystal grid and then down into Mother Earth. Connect to the Earth and visualise this energy moving up into your grid as your grid becomes connected and grounded into the Earth.

Call upon the golden light of the universe. Visualise this light streaming down into your crown chakra and then down into Mother Earth as you become a conduit. Connect to Mother Earth and breathe her energy up into your heart. Now breathe the golden light down from the universe and into your heart. Breathe these two energies into your heart centre at the same time.

Set your mind intention to activate the grid. If you are programming your grid, now is the time to set your intention for your program.

Now visualise the light and love from your heart and direct this energy into your wand, then into the grid.

Place your wand point over the anchor crystal in the centre.

Move the wand from the anchor crystal, connecting to one of the crystals on the outside of the grid, drawing a straight line.

Visualise the energy lines connecting to and from each crystal. Continue to activate the grid by following the six-pointed star lines, moving from the outside crystal to the crystal next to it. Now make your way back to the anchor crystal, then move back down the same line you just created to the same crystal on the outside. Connect to the crystal to the left in the six-pointed star, then draw the energy back into the centre crystal. Follow this format until you have activated the whole grid, working clockwise and finishing in the centre.

Visualise the energies streaming upwards out of the central crystal, spiralling the energy upwards.

Now using your voice or any other type of instrument, sound into the grid with the intention to activate and integrate the grid. Note: A good way to keep your mind clear while doing the activation is to chant this healing invocation: 'I am a clear and pure channel, love is my guide'. Or you could chant Ohm Shanti, which means 'peace'.

You can add extra crystals to the grid by placing them in the centre, making sure you don't knock any of the crystals because that will create a break in the circuit and you will have to activate the grid again. You can also place more Quartz lasers on the outside of the grid, pointing outwards to direct the grid's energies out. And you can place a circle of Hematite around the outside of the grid to ground the energies.

Crystals and chakras

Chakras are centres of energy and consciousness within our energy body. Hundreds of chakras make up our energy field; however, we commonly work with seven main chakras. They are our main focal points of life energy. The chakras indicate our evolution spiritually, emotionally, mentally and physically. When we nourish our chakras on a regular basis they begin to radiate a brilliant light that creates balance on all levels in all of our bodies — the physical, emotional, mental and spiritual. Each chakra relates to different aspects of our life and each has a different colour and vibration. When the chakras are out of balance it can create disharmony in our day-to-day life.

It is very important when working with healing that we understand the chakra system because this is where most of our energetic blockages are held. When we understand the chakras and what they represent it is easier for us to identify with the issues that are creating imbalances and where they are held or stored. This allows for more understanding and knowledge of how we can assist people in releasing and dissolving unwanted energy and balancing the chakras.

Different crystals align to and bring balance to each individual chakra, although some crystals relate to more than one chakra. The next section introduces you to the relationship between the chakras and the aligning crystals, and later in the book I introduce advanced chakra layouts.

Following is a simple breakdown of the aspects of our lives each chakra relates to, so you can start to get a deeper understanding of how this system works and relates to healing.

Base chakra

Colour: Red

Relates to:

- Security and stability
- Grounding
- Survival
- Instinct
- Money
- Material needs
- Ancestors

Crystals associated with the base chakra are Black Obsidian, Red Jasper, Hematite, Shungite, Black Tourmaline, Smoky Quartz, Petrified Wood, Goethite, Pyrite, Stibnite, Agate, Amber, Apophyllite, Chiastolite, Eudialyte, Apache Tears, Aragonite, Jet, Brown Tourmaline, Serpentine, Bloodstone, Mookaite, Shaman Stone, Boji Stone™, and Cuprite.

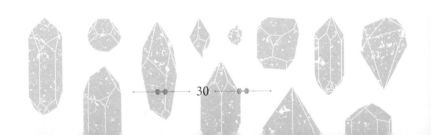

Sacral chakra

Colour: Orange

Relates to:

- Desires
- Appetites
- Addictions
- Creativity
- Relationships
- Karmic patterns
- Sexuality and sensuality
- Community, family and tribe

Crystals associated with the sacral chakra are Carnelian, Brown Tourmaline, Rutilated Quartz, Shiva Lingam, Tiger's Eye, Fire Agate, Bixbite, Crocoite, Ruby, Red Tourmaline, Agate, Amber, Apache Tears, Aragonite, Apophylite, Bloodstone, Eudialyte, Cuprite, Jet, Moonstone, Serpentine, Mookaite, Orpiment and Smoky Quartz.

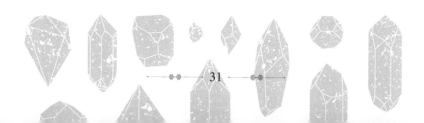

Solar plexus chakra

Colour: Yellow

Relates to:

- Empowerment
- Confidence
- Self-discipline
- Free will
- Self-esteem
- Inner strength
- Courage

Crystals associated with the solar plexus are Sunstone, Mookaite, Chrysocolla, Golden Calcite, Citrine, Heliodor, Chrysanthemum Stone, Rhodonite, Amazonite, Ametrine, Brazilianite, Cacoxenite, Chrysoberyl, Fluorite, Tiger's Eye, Orpiment, Pyromorphite, Eudialyte and Sodalite.

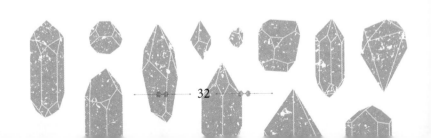

Heart chakra

Colour: Green and pink

Relates to:

- Unconditional love
- Love of self
- Compassion
- Forgiveness
- Acceptance
- Nurturing
- Receiving
- Intimacy
- Joy, laughter and happiness

Crystals that are associated with the heart are Rose Quartz, Green Aventurine, Kunzite, Rhodochrosite, Malachite, Chrysocolla, Chrysoprase, Diamond, Hiddenite, Morganite, Nirvana Quartz, Pink Tourmaline, Green Tourmaline, Watermelon Tourmaline, Prehnite, Diopside, Dioptase, Emerald, Jade, Peridot, Sugilite, Ocean Jasper, Herkimer Diamond, Serpentine, Ajoite, Angelite, Green Apatite, Turquoise, Aquamarine, Celestite, Chrysoberyl, Fluorite, Larimar, Moonstone, Pyromorphite, Vivianite.

Throat chakra

Colour: Blue
Relates to:

- Speaking your truth
- Communication
- Alignment to soul purpose
- Expression
- Creativity

Crystals associated with the throat
are Blue Lace Agate, Aquamarine,
Blue Kyanite, Ajoite, Dumortierite, Larimar, Sodalite, Blue Tourmaline,
Turquoise and Vivianite.

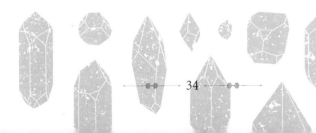

Third eye chakra

Colour: Violet

Relates to:

- Clarity and awareness
- Deepening intuition
- Visualisation
- Spiritual insight
- Dreams and visions

Crystals associated with the third eye
are Amethyst, Azurite, Lapis Lazuli,
Fluorite, Lepidolite, Tanzanite, Ametrine, Blue Apatite, Charoite,
Labradorite, Natrolite, Phenacite, Purpurite, Shattuckite Pyrite and Blue
Tourmaline.

Crown chakra

Colour: White

Relates to:

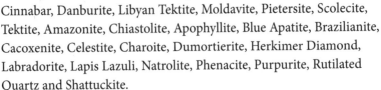

- Union with higher self
- I am presence
- Connection with source
- Divine knowledge and wisdom
- Spiritual awareness

Crystals associated with the crown are Clear Quartz, Calcite, Selenite, Angelite, Cinnabar, Danburite, Libyan Tektite, Moldavite, Pietersite, Scolecite, Tektite, Amazonite, Chiastolite, Apophyllite, Blue Apatite, Brazilianite, Cacoxenite, Celestite, Charoite, Dumortierite, Herkimer Diamond, Labradorite, Lapis Lazuli, Natrolite, Phenacite, Purpurite, Rutilated Quartz and Shattuckite.

Distance healing with crystals

Having a loving thought about someone is a form of distant healing. By setting an intention to send someone love and healing, it is done. Healing does not have to be local to work; the person you are doing healing with does not have to be in the same room. This has been proven scientifically. When we have a thought it travels around the universe and back to us at the speed of light. The same process happens with distance healing. When working with the power of intention to send the healing energy to someone or something, the intention acts like a funnel, allowing the energy to travel through space and time to reach the person you intended your intention to flow to.

Crystals have the ability to amplify energies. When working with the crystals in distance healing, the crystals will assist in amplifying the healing energy of love. When you send healing to another, it is very important to see them as already healed. See this divine soul as perfect, whole and complete as you express this to the universe with certainty.

Sending healing energy

To send healing energy, follow these steps.

Choose a pointed crystal, preferably double terminated quartz.

Guide yourself into a relaxed and centred space.

Call upon the Deva of the crystal, your Guides and Healing Angels for their love and support.

Open and allow yourself to become a channel or conduit for universal healing energy.

Say the following healing invocation three times:

I invoke the love of the divine universe within my heart

I am a clear and pure channel

Love is my guide

Close your eyes and start to focus on your breath.

Call upon the light and love of the universe, and start to breathe and draw this into your crown chakra.

Allow this healing light and love to fill every single cell of your being.

Bring your attention to your heart space, filling yourself with love.

Visualise and feel yourself shining and radiating pure love from your heart, feeling at peace and full of serenity.

Bring your crystal to your heart, and send love and compassion into the crystal.

Now visualise the person you would like to send the love to.

Working with the crystal, send and offer the love from deep within your heart, the love of the universe and the love of the Earth to this person.

See them receiving this love and see them as perfect, whole and complete, radiating, full of light. Ask that every cell in their being be brought back to perfect harmony with their higher self as you visualise their whole body full of healing energy.

Do this for as long as it feels appropriate; you will intuitively know when to stop.

To finish the healing, visualise the person in a golden sphere of light and see them merge into it. Thank your Guides and Angels.

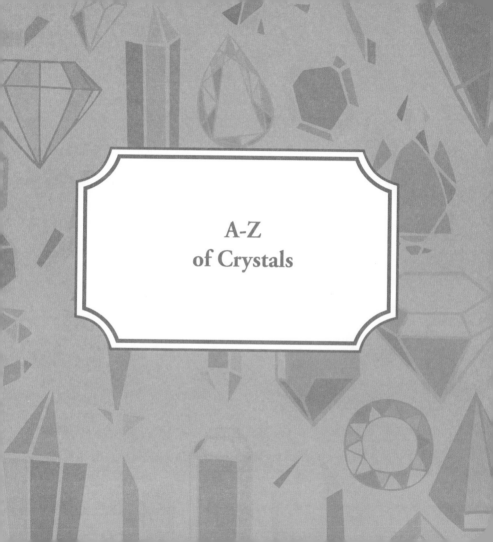

A-Z
of Crystals

Agate

Crystal colour: A range and variety of earthly colours consisting of creams, whites, blacks, browns, reds and oranges
Related chakras: Base and sacral

Crystal meaning:

- Restores, grounds and nurtures the energy field
- Provides emotional and energetic support
- Brings in all the divine qualities of Mother Earth
- Reconnects you to the divine energy flow of the planet
- Connects you deeply to Mother Earth and opens you to receive her powerful healing energy

    - Assists in shamanic journeying to meet the plant and tree Devas
    - Aligns you to their power and spirit animal helpers

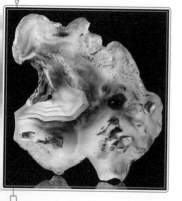

Ajoite

Crystal colour: Varieties of blues and greens
Related chakras: Heart and throat

Crystal meaning:

- Encourages you to connect deeply to your feminine energy
- Reconnects you to the ancient wisdom of the goddess
- Reconnects you to your feminine, allowing you to find the strength and wisdom of vulnerability where deep healing occurs

Amazonite

....

Crystal colour: Bluish green with white streaks
Related chakras: Solar plexus and crown

Crystal meaning:

- Aligns you to your life purpose and encourages you to step onto the path with strength and courage
- Assists you in finding the divine truth in all things
- Facilitates deep internal reflection
- Encourages you to come into alignment with your divine will, manifesting your heart's desires

Amber

Crystal colour: Various shades of translucent orange
Related chakras: Base and sacral

Crystal meaning:

- Allows a deeper connection to the nature and tree spirits
- Draws disease from the body
- Assists in dissolving old patterns from the past that are handed down through the DNA and family
- Assists in creating a deep connection with your ancestors to receive their deep wisdom of life

Amethyst

Crystal colour: Various shades of translucent purple
Related chakra: Third eye

Crystal meaning:

- Powerful overall healing crystal, which assists on all levels
- Balances the left and right hemispheres of the brain, allowing you to enter into deep meditation and relaxation
- Overcomes all types of addiction, bringing awareness and healing to the core issue held beneath the addiction and dissolving the old patterns
- Opens you to your psychic abilities
- Assists wonderfully in dream recall
- Aids in anxiety and stress relief
- Soothes energetically and emotionally

Amethyst Awakening (Amethyst Elestial)

Crystal colour: Translucent purple mixed with smoky quartz
Related chakras: All

Crystal meaning:

- This beautiful crystal is from the same family as the Awakening Crystal (Elestial); however, is formed with Amethyst
- One of the most powerful and potent crystals on the planet, here to assist in healing all forms of trauma
- Helps you to move through lifelong addictions and patterns as you awaken to the core issues that created the need for addiction
- Assists deep spiritual awakening
- Supports and enhances emotional intelligence and balances the emotions

Ametrine

Crystal colour: Various shades of golds and purples
Related chakras: Solar plexus and third eye

Crystal meaning:

- Assists in finding a deeper space for meditation and relaxation
- Opens the third eye and activates your deeper intuition
- Stimulates and revitalises the brain, enhancing memory
- Invokes personal power and inner strength

Angelite

Crystal colour: Pale shades of blue and grey
Related chakras: Heart and crown

Crystal meaning:

- Aligns us to the Angelic Realm, where we receive healing and divine guidance
- Attracts new people and friendships into your life that align with your higher purpose
- Connects us to the spirit world and the wisdom it has to offer

Apache Tears

Crystal colour: Black
Related chakras: Base and sacral

Crystal meaning:

- Assists in dissolving fear of moving forward and of change
- Allows you to connect to and release any wounds around grief and fear
- Encourages you to stay centred and grounded and to see the light at the end of the tunnel, bringing hope
- Assists in overcoming and working through fear of death, accidents and injury

Apatite – Blue

Crystal colour: Blue
Related chakras: Third eye and throat

Crystal meaning:

- Stimulates and awakens the third eye to receive clearer vision and insight, acting as a powerful visionary stone
- Aids in positive communication
- Clears and activates the throat chakra

Apatite – Green

Crystal colour: Green
Related chakra: Heart

Crystal meaning:

- Overall gentle, supportive healing crystal
- Awakens the loving essence of the heart
- Supports in realising and dissolving unhealthy eating patterns and addictions

Apophyllite

Crystal colour: Various colours
Related chakras: Sacral, base and crown

Crystal meaning:

- Assists in healing past life issues, awakening wisdom and understanding of the past
- Supports in realising and releasing old karmic contracts and connections that no longer serve you
- Assists in addressing and letting go of karmic issues such as vows of poverty, silence and chastity
- Deepens your connection to family, promoting healing of family wounds
- Integrates past life wisdom

Aquamarine

Crystal colour: A range of translucent and opaque blues and aqua
Related chakras: Heart and throat

Crystal meaning:

- Facilitates clear communication, allowing you to speak truth from the heart and supporting self-expression
- Assists in connecting to and expressing your own wisdom and knowledge
    - Allows you to find your voice
    - Soothes and calms the emotions
    - Awakens the divine feminine
    - Dissolves the need to feel defensive

Aragonite

Crystal colour: Orange and brown
Related chakras: Base and sacral

Crystal meaning:

- Brings deep awareness and healing to suppressed emotions
- Unlocks the hidden aspects of the human psyche
- Assists in connecting to and understanding the deep wisdom held within the emotional body, bringing about emotional maturity

Aventurine

Crystal colour: Various shades of green
Related chakra: Heart

Crystal meaning:

- Assists in connecting to and healing deep wounds and patterns from your childhood
- Heals and soothes painful emotions held within the heart
- Assists those who are highly sensitive
- Nurtures the inner child in times of deep healing
- Allows you to acknowledge the loving, joyful child within
- Allows you to balance any insensitivity in your life, bringing in a deeper level of compassion
- Encourages understanding and insight behind emotional issues

Azurite

Crystal colour: Vibrant ranges of blues
Related chakra: Third eye

Crystal meaning:

- Connects to and enhances your intuition, creating trust to follow your own guidance
- Expands your awareness and allows you to see things from a different perspective, allowing for transformation and healing to occur and letting go of old wounds and belief systems
- Dissolves old belief systems, concepts and misperceptions
- Opens you to clear vision and insight into your life and others

Bixbite

. . . .

Crystal colour: Opaque to translucent reds
Related chakras: Sacral

Crystal meaning:

- Enhances and invokes pleasure and passion within your life, allowing divine union and deep sexual connection to your beloved
- Invites you to explore the sacredness and power of your sexuality
- Awakens romantic love and passion
- Strengthens sexual partnerships and deep connections, creating a sacred space for tantric union
  - Stimulates your sexual energy and invokes healing of any old wounds held from past traumatic experiences around sexual intimacy

Bloodstone

Crystal colour: Dark greens with red and orange spots
Related chakras: Base and sacral

Crystal meaning:

- Purifies the blood and any blood disorders
- Restores and nourishes the body
- Centres, balances and reconnects you to yourself
- Invites you onto the path of self-love and care
- Allows you to connect to the innate healing energy of the physical body, supporting it to heal itself

Blue Lace Agate

Crystal colour: Pale blue with white swirls and streaks
Related chakra: Throat

Crystal meaning:

- Assists in creating clear communication and speaking your divine truth
- Aids in positive communication
- Helps you to go with the flow of life
- Enhances relaxation
- Opens the throat chakra
- Enhances self-expression
- Promotes peaceful flow of expression and calmness

Boji Stones™

Crystal colour: Grey stones. Boji Stones™ always come in pairs. The smooth stone represents the feminine energy and the rough stone represents the masculine energy

Related chakras: All

Crystal meaning:

- Creates balance
- Grounds the spiritual experience into the physical world
- Supports soul retrieval journey to the inner realms
- Assists in connecting to your power animal in spirit

Brazilianite

....

Crystal colour: A range of translucent to opaque greens
Related chakras: Solar plexus and crown

Crystal meaning:

- Assists in decision making
- Supports you to become more assertive
- Enhances intuition
- Brings inner peace and self-awareness
- Enhances flexibility in your life
- Assists in enhancing creative projects
- Self-empowerment

Brookite

. . . .

Crystal colour: Various shades of browns, golds and yellows
Related chakras: All

Crystal meaning:

- Enhances insight into self and others
- Brings lightness, and uplifts the soul and spirit
- Assists those who live with fear of the future to live more in the present

Bustamite

....

Crystal colour: Various shades of pink with white
Related chakras: Heart and solar plexus

Crystal meaning:

- Initiation crystal used in ceremonies and rites of passage
- Strengthens belief in self and creates a sense of belonging
- Heals and transforms issues of the heart (used by shamans in South America for this purpose)

Cacoxenite

....

Crystal colour: A variety of golds, browns and blacks
Related chakras: Solar plexus and crown

Crystal meaning:

- Great for enhancing your channelling gifts and abilities
- Enhances creative ideas and awakens imagination
- Facilitates high vibrational healing work
- Journeys with you into the magical realm of spirit
- Activates new ideas and inspiration in your life

Calcite

Crystal colour: All
Related chakras: All

Crystal meaning:

- Strengthens the bones and skeletal system
- Dissolves stress from your life
- Brings inner peace and tranquility
- Calms the mind and balances the heart
- Facilitates states of deep relaxation and meditation

Calcite – Golden

Crystal colour: Range of opaque yellow to gold
Related chakras: All

Crystal meaning:

- Opens the crown chakra, and draws in the light and love of the universe
- Promotes deep relaxation and calms the mind
- Illuminates the soul
- Connects you deeply and fully to the wisdom of the cosmos

Carnelian

Crystal colour: Various hues of orange
Related chakra: Sacral

Crystal meaning:

- Assists in healing and moving through sexual issues, and promotes healthy sexual relationships
- Assists in working through co-dependent issues and letting go of negative attachments
- Assists you to become more independent
- Transforms anger into motivation and creativity
- Enhances and awakens creativity within the soul
- Promotes and assists you to step into courage

Celestite

Crystal colour: Translucent to opaque blue
Related chakras: Throat and crown

Crystal meaning:

- Facilitates a deep connection to the divine source
- Encourages acceptance of the flow of life and that all is in divine order
- Facilitates deep soul healing and transformation
- Creates a space of peace, calm, tranquillity and deep relaxation
- Assists connection and communication with the Angelic Realm
- Soothes the emotions, allowing the heart to open

Charoite

....

Crystal colour: Various shades of swirling purples, whites and black
Related chakras: Third eye and crown

Crystal meaning:

- Enhances your psychic abilities and gifts
- Advances spiritual growth and transformation
- Allows you to expand through self-denial to see the truth
- Deepens your journey on the spiritual path
- Assists in finding the answers that lie within, creating self-empowerment

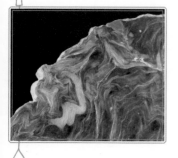

Chiastolite (Andalusite)

Crystal colour: Various hues and shades of golds, browns, oranges, blacks and whites; often seen with a black cross through the crystal
Related chakras: Base and crown

Crystal meaning:

- Brings you into alignment with the powerful healing energy and vibration of the Earth
- Invokes and anchors the truth of your wisdom to live this in your day-to-day life
- Enhances the strength and assurance of your light and wisdom

Chrysanthemum Stone

Crystal colour: Black with white feathers that look like a flower
Related chakra: Solar plexus

Crystal meaning:

- Bringer and enhancer of abundance
- Allows you to blossom in your fullness
- Brings light and understanding to your inner darkness or denial
- Holds the energy of the yin and yang, facilitating balance and harmony

Chrysoberyl

Crystal colour: Translucent to opaque green
Related chakras: Heart and solar plexus

Crystal meaning:

- Allows you to attain self-mastery, letting your true essence shine through
- Creates truth, confidence and freedom in your life
- Aligns the divine heart and mind to a higher purpose
- Assists you to find the inner strength and determination to follow your passion, moving out of the old, comfortable place and to bathing and shining in the new of your totality
- Encourages you to listen to your inner voice
- Encourages you to embrace personal wisdom and enhances personal growth

Chrysocolla

Crystal colour: Various shades of greens and blues
Related chakras: Solar plexus and heart

Crystal meaning:

- Assists in bringing eternal love and connection to the divine feminine
- Assists in connecting to the sacred goddess within
- Brings old emotion to the surface for transmutation in a gentle, supporting way, letting go of old trauma
- Encourages honouring of self and others' choices and decisions
- Assists in powerful, clear communication of our feelings, creating unconditional love and understanding of situations

Chrysoprase

Crystal colour: Green
Related chakra: Heart

Crystal meaning:

- Encourages appropriate self-discipline in your life
- Addresses and assists in bringing awareness and healing to self-sacrificing behaviours
- Assists in resolving inner conflict and turmoil
- Assists in nurturing, love and support of self
- Helps in healing old pain residue from abusive and toxic situations

Cinnabar

....

Crystal colour: Various shades of red and browns with white
Related chakra: Crown

Crystal meaning:

- Allows you to get out of your own way
- Allows you to trust in the flow of life and what it has to offer
- Invites the energy of joy and magic into your life on all levels
- Encourages you to lighten up and remember to play and have fun in life
- Invites you to choose a positive outlook on life

Citrine

Crystal colour: Yellows and golds
Related chakra: Solar plexus

Crystal meaning:

- Purification crystal on all levels
- Assists in manifesting wealth and abundance
- Brings healthy positive energy into your life
- Shifts old patterns of lack and negativity
- Brings in the joy and magic of life

Crocoite

. . . .

Crystal colour: Vibrant orange
Related chakra: Sacral

Crystal meaning:

- Has aphrodisiac qualities
- Activates the Kundalini energy
- Invokes your deep sexual and life force energy
- Deepens our connection to our sensuality
- Assists in sexual healing
- Enhances Tantric union
- Enhances sexual confidence
- Assists you in expressing your creativity

Chrysotile

Crystal colour: Green with white shimmery lines
Related chakras: Base and crown

Crystal meaning:

- Allows you to connect deeply with your power animal in spirit
- Allows deep connection to the inner worlds
- Assists in awakening the wisdom of the animal kingdom and the deep healing it has to share

Cuprite

Crystal colour: Deep red
Related chakras: Base and sacral

Crystal meaning:

- Supports exploring the shadow self; also healing deep issues related to the sacred feminine as you are supported to enter into your own personal healing cave for self-reflection
- Provides access to sacred ancient knowledge of the feminine; used also for rites of passage

- Supports and holds you as you enter into the void, a journey that needs to be taken for deep transformational healing
- Supports you to feel like you belong here on Earth

Danburite

Crystal colour: Translucent to opaque
Related chakra: Crown

Crystal meaning:

- Deepens connection to your higher self
- Deepens connection to your soul purpose and potential
- Creates a deep sense of stillness and inner peace
- Connects you with your limitless potential to create your deepest desires
- Enhances your spirituality, psychic development and channelling abilities
- Facilitates access to the higher realms and connection to the Angels and ascended masters

Diamond

....

Crystal colour: Translucent to opaque yellows and golds
Related chakra: Heart

Crystal meaning:

- Brings light to any situation
- Dispels anger and promotes love and peace
- Promotes deep connection and intimacy with your partner, creating a loving, divine union
- Deepens intimate relationships

- Encourages you to connect deeply to your sensuality
- Promotes unconditional love and deep commitment
- Brings the awareness that we are all one and all love
- Allows you to feel safe in your vulnerability

Diopside

Crystal colour: Various hues of green
Related chakra: Heart

Crystal meaning:

- Assists in connecting to the heart of Mother Earth, realising she is our true divine mother, receiving healing energy around our mother issues
- Allows an opening to receive and nurture yourself
- Brings awareness to deep-seated rejection issues that stem from birth or early childhood
- Assists in releasing fear and abandonment
- Assists you in identifying trauma carried from the womb
- Assists in healing issues in connecting and bonding with your inner child or your own children

Dioptase

Crystal colour: Emerald green
Related chakra: Heart

Crystal meaning:

- Heals the inner realms of the wounded heart and enhances openness in your life
- Transmutes and heals emotional pain and old wounds of the past, as the green healing ray penetrates deep into the heart chakra
- Allows you to release and dissolve sadness in your life
- Encourages you to let down the walls of anger, bitterness and resistance, and embrace love and connection with others
- Helps release emotionally defensive behaviours and opens the heart for healing

Dumortierite

Crystal colour: Variety of blues, white and black
Related chakras: Throat and crown

Crystal meaning:

- Allows you to communicate divine spiritual teachings in a practical and grounded way so that others will understand clearly
- Supports you to integrate and believe in the wisdom and knowledge received from your higher self
- Assists you in addressing and releasing any old blockages around expressing your spiritual truths and wisdom

Emerald

....

Crystal colour: Opaque to translucent greens
Related chakra: Heart

Crystal meaning:

- Promotes Divine Love and compassion
- Assists in staying connected to the wisdom of the heart
- Deeply activates the heart chakra and assists in creating intimacy with self, others and the divine
- Assists in letting go of old connections and superficial relationships that no longer serve you

- Invokes the magical healing energy of the dragon
- Releases the need to please others
- Brings in positive self-image and supports you to feel good about yourself

Eudialyte

Crystal colour: Ruby red mixed with grey and black
Related chakras: Solar plexus and sacral

Crystal meaning:

- Restores your self-respect
- Assists in finding a deep respect and honour for yourself
- Enhances self-acceptance
- Teaches you to put yourself first in a healthy way
- Awakens your deep passion and spark for life

Fairy Stone

Crystal colour: Light grey to dark grey stone
Related chakras: All

Crystal meaning:

- Sacred stone to the Native American tribes found in Northern Quebec, Canada; also a stone of magic and good luck
- Enhances fertility
- Assists in healing trauma created in the womb
- Offers protection
- Brings good health and prosperity

Fire Agate

Crystal colour: Variety of vibrant rich colours of red, orange, black, cream, brown, green, blue, gold and yellow

Related chakra: Sacral

Crystal meaning:

- Assists in dissolving blocks around your artistic gifts and talents, allowing you to open and shine in deep passion and creativity
- Enhances self-confidence
- Encourages you to get in touch with your dynamic nature
- Assists you to move forward with passion and positivity
- Deepens your passion and spark for life, fuelling your internal flame and invoking inspiration
- Stimulates and balances sexual energy

Fluorite

Crystal colour: Range of purple, green and yellow
Related chakras: All

Crystal meaning:

- Allows you to open to new knowledge and stimulates learning
- Stimulates the mental body and enhances memory and decision making
- Assists in releasing unwanted thought patterns and distractions
- Supports you when you are experiencing emotional confusion to gain a clear perspective
- Releases constant worry and invites you into the present moment
- Aids in vision and deep insight
- Balances the mind and mental body

Fulgurite

Crystal colour: Whites, browns and creams
Related chakras: All

Crystal meaning:

- Activates and facilitates the Kundalini activation within the physical body
- Powerfully and quickly clears old emotional patterns
- Promotes deep transformation

Galena

. . . .

Crystal colour: Grey to silver
Related chakras: All

Crystal meaning:

- Very strong grounding stone, creating courage and strength
- Promotes and supports soul retrieval journeys
- Balances and heals the nervous system and balances blood pressure

Garnet

. . . .

Crystal colour: Deep red, black, brown, yellow and green
Related chakras: All

Crystal meaning:

- Promotes balance and stability in your life
- Enhances personal power
- Creates overall health and wellbeing
- Allows you to dissolve commitment issues and create deeper, fulfilling relationships
- Encourages you to connect deeply to your sensuality
- Helps you address issues of self-doubt
- Teaches you to trust and believe in yourself
- Connects to and draws up the healing energy of the Earth

Goethite

....

Crystal colour: Various hues of brownish black, yellows and reds
Related chakra: Base

Crystal meaning:

- Accesses the sacred wisdom that lies within the Earth
- Balances, stimulates and heals the emotional body
- Allows you to feel and deal with your grief
- Overcomes lack of faith in self and humanity
- Supports you to overcome helplessness

Heliodor

....

Crystal colour: Translucent to opaque gold and yellow
Related chakra: Solar plexus

Crystal meaning:

- Allows you to take more responsibility in your life
- Promotes flexibility and spontaneity, and trust in the universal order and divine plan
- Allows you to let go of control created by ego and allows more flexibility and motivation in your life
- Encourages self-empowerment and strength

Hematite

Crystal colour: Various shades of black to grey
Related chakra: Base

Crystal meaning:

- Purifies and cleanses
- Cleanses the blood and assists in healing blood disorders
- Grounds and connects to the centre of the Earth, enhancing manifestation skills
- Promotes balance
- Encourages gentle healing after shock or trauma
- Assists in integration of sudden and unexpected change

Herkimer Diamond

Crystal colour: Translucent to opaque
Related chakras: Heart and crown

Crystal meaning:

- Invokes your dynamic personality and vibrancy
- Allows you to shine in your totality and magnificence
- Draws in vibrant energy
- Energetically detoxifies
- Activates inspiration and new ideas, and clears creative blocks
- Sweeps the mind clear of clutter
- Revitalises the spirit

Hiddenite

. . . .

Crystal colour: Translucent to opaque green
Related chakra: Heart

Crystal meaning:

- Crystal of deep gratitude
- Allows you to realise that gratitude is the key to receiving
- Opens the heart and assists in dissolving any judgments in your life
- Allows you to create a sense of satisfaction and fulfilment in your life
- Helps shift unhealthy patterns such as comfort eating and other addictive behaviours
- Encourages appreciation for life and yourself

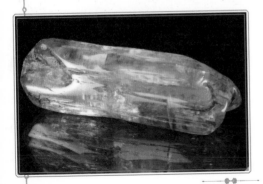

Jade

. . . .

Crystal colour: Various shades of green
Related chakra: Heart

Crystal meaning:

- Creates abundance and good fortune
- Promotes positive thinking and self-expression
- Creates inner harmony
- Promotes trust in the creative power of the universe
- Encourages faith in the ebb and flow of life
- Enhances devotion to yourself and your life

Jasper – Mookaite

Crystal colour: Various earthly colours such as oranges, reds, purples, browns, yellows and creams
Related chakras: Base and sacral

Crystal meaning:

- Used in ceremonies and rituals
- Encourages deep connection to the wisdom and ancestors of Australia
- Helps release deep emotions such as fear and anger
- Assists in your journey into the spirit world and Dreamtime
- Helps us receive deep healing from the Earth
- Reconnects us to the heart of the Earth
  - Grounds and protects us
  - Assists in healing issues related to the liver

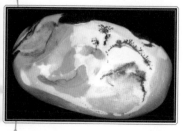

Jasper – Ocean

Crystal colour: Various colours of green, red, orange, yellow, cream, white and brown

Related chakras: Base, sacral and heart

Crystal meaning:

- Assists in healing any suppressed emotions, bringing them to the surface for transformation
- Allows you to open and receive
- Connects us to the healing energy of the ocean
- Assists in the release of deeply held, long-term anger, rage, resentment and grief
- Heals current emotional trauma
- Helps to dissolve the emotional walls of protection that prevent true healing

Jasper – Red

Crystal colour: Red
Related chakra: Base

Crystal meaning:

- Sacred stone used in ceremonies and rituals for protection
- Connects us to Mother Earth and draws her healing energy up into the body, creating strength and balance
- Connects us with our ancestors
- Assists us to set healthy boundaries
  - Awakens ancient memories
  - Assists in overcoming deep-seated fear of abandonment
  - Assists in letting go of controlling behaviours

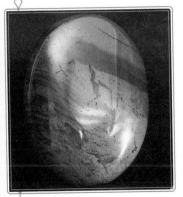

Jet

......

Crystal colour: Black
Related chakras: Base and sacral

Crystal meaning:

- Assists in entering the void where we obtain our true depth of self, gaining understanding and power
- Assists in embracing disowned aspects of self
- Stimulates and awakens the Kundalini
- Helps to clear and dissolve energetic residue within the head, clearing headaches

Kunzite

. . . .

Crystal colour: Various hues of pink, purple, cream and white
Related chakra: Heart

Crystal meaning:

- Connects you to your own infinite source of love
- Allows the heart to expand as you enter into the flow of giving and receiving
- Activates the wisdom of love in the deeper chambers of the heart
- Allows you to heal from abandonment and rejection as you find your own source of deep love from within

- Opens and aligns the heart chakra to Divine Love
- Assists in dissolving deeply held pain and resentment
- Brings awareness to behaviours and patterns of self-betrayal

Kyanite – Blue

Crystal colour: Blue with strips of silver mica
Related chakra: Throat

Crystal meaning:

- Deepens self-awareness
- Expands your consciousness, creating new opportunities in life
- Allows you to let go of old emotions, allowing you to express the old and make way for the new
- Helps you in letting go and moving with the ebb and flow of life
- Assists in connecting to your voice with free-flowing expression

Labradorite

Crystal colour: Greys and silver with vibrant blues and greens
Related chakras: Third eye and crown

Crystal meaning:

- Allows you to connect to the mystery and magic of life
- Assists in awakening the magic of your soul
- Brings deep awareness of our spiritual knowledge, allowing it to manifest in your day-to-day life
- Brings spiritual insight
- Supports you to integrate spiritual experiences into the physical world
- Opens and activates the third eye

Lapis Lazuli

Crystal colour: Various shades of blue with gold streaks and speckles
Related chakras: Third eye and crown

Crystal meaning:

- Powerful spiritual initiation stone, awakening spiritual wisdom and knowledge from within
- Opens you to clairvoyance
- Supports past life awareness and healing of any karmic patterns
- Attunes you to your ancient wisdom
- Enhances psychic gifts and awareness
- Supports you in connecting to your deep spiritual truths
- Severs karmic ties

Larimar

. . . .

Crystal colour: Various shades of bluish greens and white
Related chakras: Throat and heart

Crystal meaning:

- Empowers the goddess within all of us, allowing for deep healing of our feminine
- Balances the fire and water element, soothing the emotions and setting us free from anger and frustration
- Calms and stabilises erratic emotional states
- Brings comfort and support in cases of heightened sensitivity
- Assists reactive individuals to express from a place of self-empowerment
- Relaxes the nerves

Lepidolite

Crystal colour: Pinks and light purples
Related chakras: Third eye and sacral

Crystal meaning:

- Assists in letting go of old critical judgments of self
- Assists in transitioning from the old way of being to creating a new path of self-empowerment
- Allows us to see the truth and live in the moment
- Assists us in surrendering and creating more peace and serenity in our life
- Supports perfectionists in letting go
- Soothes the inner critic
- Releases unrealistic expectations of self and others

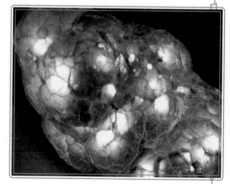

Libyan Gold Tektite

Crystal colour: Opaque yellow and gold
Related chakra: Crown

Crystal meaning:

- Powerful manifestation crystal
- Assists in connecting to light beings from other galaxies and dimensions
- Releases fear of the unknown, allowing more trust in your life
- Dissolves fear around extraterrestrial beings

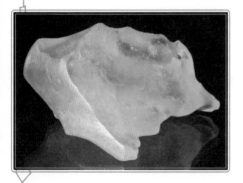

Malachite

Crystal colour: Green with black swirls
Related chakras: All

Crystal meaning:

- Deep physical healing crystal that penetrates into all levels of your being and promotes overall healing
- Powerful crystal that assists in healing broken bones, bruises and all physical disease
- Opens and expands the heart chakra, allowing the power of love to dissolve deeply held resentment and sadness stored within the body
- Excellent to work with after meditation or healing to integrate the experience
- Eases deep heartache

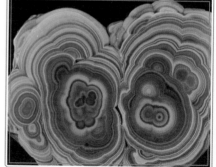

Malachite and Azurite

Crystal colour: Green with black swirls mixed with vibrant blue
Related chakras: All

Crystal meaning:

- This crystal is Malachite and Azurite growing together to create a powerful synergy
- Holds the energetic properties of both Malachite and Azurite, with both crystals amplifying the other to create a powerful overall healing crystal on all levels
- Activates the blue and green rays of peace and healing
- Refer to Malachite and Azurite for properties

Malachite and Chrysocolla

Crystal colour: Green with black swirls and various shades of greens and blues

Related chakras: All

Crystal meaning:

- This crystal is Malachite and Chrysocolla growing together to create powerful synergy
- Holds the energetic properties of both Malachite and Chrysocolla, with both crystals amplifying each other to create a powerful overall healing crystal on all levels
- Refer to Malachite and Chrysocolla for properties

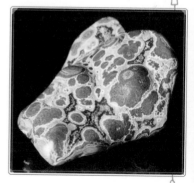

Moldavite

Crystal colour: Opaque bottle green
Related chakra: Crown

Crystal meaning:

- Powerful crystal that assists in connecting and communicating with dimensional light beings from other universes and planes of existence
- Brings deep spiritual connection to awakening and healing
- Supports astral travelling into different time, places and dimensions

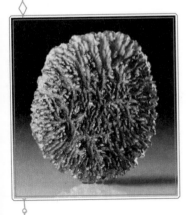

Moonstone

....

Crystal colour: Varieties of white, pearly and cream hues
Related chakras: Sacral and heart

Crystal meaning:

- Connects us deeply to our feminine and heals any imbalances in this area
- Enhances fertility, planting new seeds, ideas and inspirations
- Creates new beginnings, new directions and creativity
- Connects us to the energy of the moon and her cycles, bringing us into balance and the ebb and flow of life
- Encourages us to be open to intimacy
- Assists in birthing new projects and creations

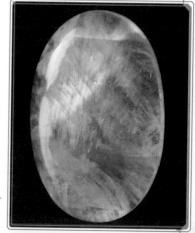

Morganite

Crystal colour: Opaque to translucent pink
Related chakra: Heart

Crystal meaning:

- Creates a sacred space to assist moving deeply into the inner chambers of the heart, connecting to the love of the divine
- Enhances love of all aspects of self
- Allows you to heal old relationship wounds as the heart opens and healing occurs

  - Creates a sacred space to heal any wounds or disconnection between two souls in divine relationship
  - Assists in rapid heart healing

Natrolite

Crystal colour: Translucent to opaque yellow, brown and cream
Related chakras: Third eye and crown

Crystal meaning:

- Assists spiritual awakening
- Deepens spiritual connection
- Supports and integrates energetic and vibrational shifts
- Brings stability and energetic balance

Nirvana Quartz

Crystal colour: Opaque pink
Related chakras: Heart and crown

Crystal meaning:

- Connects deeply to the heart chakra and allows for any old wounds to be released softly and gently as you love and nurture yourself through the process
- Assists in deepening feelings of self-worth and acceptance
- Connects into the wisdom and sacred energy of the Himalayas

  where this beautiful crystal is birthed, connecting into the energy of oneness
- Assists deep meditation and stillness
- Allows you to open and blossom like a lotus flower, embodying peace and tranquility

Nuummite

Crystal colour: Black with gold and brown streaks
Related chakras: All

Crystal meaning:

- Stone of the warrior and shaman
- Supports us on the journey into our shadow self, creating a sacred space to obtain deep wisdom, strength and courage
- Increases strength and endurance during difficult times
- Assists us on the journey to self-mastery

Obsidian – Black

Crystal colour: Black
Related chakra: Base

Crystal meaning:

- Powerful cleanser of negative energy in the body and energy field
- Draws to the surface any unresolved issues for release and healing
- Dissolves destructive patterns
- Allows old habits and traits to surface so you can love and accept the self in its totality
- Allows you to enter into the void to receive wisdom and knowledge from your shadow side

- Supports you through the dark night of the soul
- Brings deep life revelations and realisations
- Brings rapid positive change

Opal

Crystal colour: Range of opaque colours
Related chakras: All

Crystal meaning:

- Allows you to experience the love, joy and pure essence of your soul
- Used in Aboriginal Dreamtime ceremonies to support and strengthen vision quests
- Activates the thymus and allows you to enter into a sacred space of love and joy
- Enhances joy, spontaneity and flow
- Encourages you to engage in the vibrant energy of life

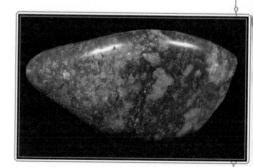

Orpiment

Crystal colour: Deep orange surrounded by gold and yellow shards
Related chakra: Sacral

Crystal meaning:

- Manifestation crystal
- Awakens new projects and ideas and allows you to connect to them
- Aligns to success in your life
- Assists in holding and staying focused on clear positive intentions
- Supports strength and commitment to self

Peridot

. . . .

Crystal colour: Opaque green
Related chakra: Heart

Crystal meaning:

- A great crystal to assist us in connecting to the nature spirits and fairy realm
- A powerful crystal for attracting abundance
- Allows us to feel deep gratitude in our life
- Enhances love, marriage and romantic ceremonies
- Deepens loyalty and commitment
- Enhances our ability to experience both inner and outer beauty
- Activates the higher heart chakra, allowing us to live in a constant state of love

Petrified Wood

Crystal colour: Crystallised wood
Related chakra: Base

Crystal meaning:

- Strong grounding stone and centring crystal
- Assists in connecting you with the tree spirits to receive deep wisdom and healing from our ancestors
- Awakens the deep knowledge that lies within the blood and bones of our ancestry
  - Assists in realising any old ancestral karma brought down through the bloodline

Phenacite

Crystal colour: Opaque to translucent
Related chakras: Third eye and crown

Crystal meaning:

- Used in spiritual awakening, initiation and ceremony
- Opens and activates the crown chakra, allowing you to access and align to universal love and wisdom
- Helps you receive divine guidance and direction from your higher self
- Enhances your spiritual journey
- Connects you to the higher realms of consciousness
- Assists in healing spiritual traumas

Pietersite

Crystal colour: Range of many earthly colours like browns, golds, reds, purples and yellows
Related chakra: Crown

Crystal meaning:

- Is the key to Heaven, enhancing your connection to higher spiritual wisdom and knowledge
- Frees you from the entrapments of the mind
- Assists in accessing the Akashic Records
  - Creates clarity and inner strength
  - Supports your spiritual awakening

Prehnite

Crystal colour: Opaque green with white
Related chakra: Heart

Crystal meaning:

- Connects us deeply into the heart of Mother Earth where we receive deep healing and nurturing
- Heals the deep inner realms of the heart, allowing you to feel safe to love again
- Supports in the rebuilding of trust in a relationship
- Encourages you to believe in yourself and your dreams
- Activates the wisdom of the heart and mind

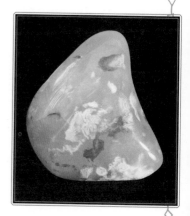

Purpurite

Crystal colour: Purplish silver
Related chakras: Third eye and crown

Crystal meaning:

- Visionary stone
- Awakens awareness of spiritual truths
- Activates deep personal insights
- Opens you to your destiny
- Builds trust in self and intuition

Pyrite

Crystal colour: Silver, gold and grey
Related chakras: Third eye and base

Crystal meaning:

- Anchors the mental body into the physical plane and assists in calming the mind, dissolving mind chatter
- Enhances brain function and memory
- Helps calm excessive thinking and irrational fears
- Allows you to create action and manifestation in your life

Pyromorphite

Crystal colour: Lime green
Related chakras: Solar plexus and heart

Crystal meaning:

- Assists in creating more patience, allowing for a deeper level of tolerance and understanding
- Deepens your intuition and gut feelings
- Encourages assertiveness and courage
- Supports you to stand up for yourself
  - Addresses issues of low self-esteem
  - Promotes a deeper belief in and respect for your self

Quartz – Clear

Crystal colour: Opaque to translucent
Related chakras: All

Crystal meaning:

- Amplifies, stores, transmutes, transcends and retains energy
- Moves light and energy into and out of the body as it clears and cleanses the energy field
- Motivates
- Enhances and amplifies intentions
- Amplifies and deepens the love and wisdom from the universe
- Allows a deep sense of clarity in your life

Rhodochrosite

Crystal colour: Pink with white swirls
Related chakra: Heart

Crystal meaning:

- Powerful crystal for self-healing and acceptance
- Brings in the energy of unconditional love to assist in balancing, soothing and healing the emotions
- Creates a deeper belief in your life, enhancing self-love and compassion
- Supports those who are emotionally overwhelmed
- Assists you to surrender and let go
- Assists you to become more self-aware
- Supports you to make balanced, rational decisions

Rhodonite

Crystal colour: Various pinks, reds and greys
Related chakras: Solar plexus and heart

Crystal meaning:

- Crystal for self-reflection
- Connect to your inner voice
- Powerful meditation crystal, allowing you to go within, creating a deeper awareness of self and allowing you to access personal power
- Helps to calm jealous and possessive feelings in relationships

Rose Quartz

Crystal colour: Various shades of pink
Related chakra: Heart

Crystal meaning:

- Crystal for deepening self-love and acceptance
- Activates deep love and peace within the heart
- Bringing unconditional love to the emotions, activating the wisdom of the heart
- Enhances compassion, gentleness and nurturing of your soul

- Brings self-fulfilment and inner peace
- Assists in creating more patience and understanding in your life
- Gently assists you to feel your inner emotions
- Supports and nurtures those going through divorce and separation

Ruby

Crystal colour: Deep shades of red
Related chakra: Sacral

Crystal meaning:

- Dissolves deep trauma and grief within the body and allows for you to love yourself through the challenges of life
- Enhances passion in all areas of life
- Deepens your sensual aspects of self, allowing you to receive a flow of life-force energy and creativity
- Helps to recognise the source of fear and anxiety

Rutilated Quartz

Crystal colour: Quartz with fine hairs inside the crystal
Related chakras: Sacral and crown

Crystal meaning:

- Assists in healing issues related to family, handed down through the DNA
- Assists in the release of fear and anxiety stemming from childhood memories
- Transforms and shifts conflicts within the family unit

Scolecite

Crystal colour: White
Related chakra: Crown

Crystal meaning:

- Enhances a deep sacred space of meditation and relaxation
- Promotes inner peace and tranquility
- Supports us in the awakening of our inner wisdom
- Allows us to access deeply held subconscious memories for transformation
- Assists in purification and illumination of the soul

Selenite

Crystal colour: White to translucent with striations
Related chakra: Crown

Crystal meaning:

- Powerful crystal working as a vacuum cleaner to purify and cleanse the aura
- Opens and stimulates the crown chakra and brings in the divine light of the cosmos, balancing the chakras
  - Encourages you to take powerful action in your life
  - Allows you to move forward in strength
  - Connects to your higher self and 'I am presence'
  - Shields the aura from any unwanted influences
  - Detoxifies the energy field

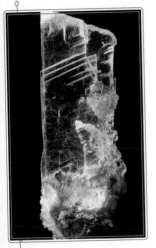

Seraphinite

Crystal colour: Green, black and white swirls
Related chakras: All

Crystal meaning:

- Quickens your spiritual learning
- Assists in connecting to the Angels and guides
- Assists in understanding and release of old emotional patterns, allowing transformation in your life
- Enhances clarity and purification
- Brings new vision and direction
- Renews your sense of purpose and life mission

Serpentine

Crystal colour: Green and black
Related chakras: Base, sacral and heart

Crystal meaning:

- Has deep connection to Peru and the ancient wisdom of its tribes and their healing ways
- Powerful healing energy that penetrates on all levels
- Stimulates the Kundalini energy to be released within the body
- Invokes deep transformation, and brings in the medicine of the snake and life-force energy

Shaman Stone

Crystal colour: Roundish, grey, iron-coated sandstone
Related chakras: All

Crystal meaning:

- A powerful ally for shamans
- Assists and facilitates shamanic and soul retrieval journeys into the three worlds
- Has deep connection to the medicine and wisdom of the Earth
- Awakens your inner shamanic power and wisdom
- Connects to your ancestors and their wisdom
- Assists in realising unwanted spirits and energetic attachments

Shattuckite

Crystal colour: Various shades of blues and greens
Related chakras: Heart, throat and crown

Crystal meaning:

- Invokes the wisdom of the inner teacher
- Opens the heart to allow you to share wisdom from a place of love
- Supports you to share the divine wisdom of the universe
- Connects you to your teacher guides in the higher realms

Shiva Lingam

Crystal colour: Brown, red, grey egg-shaped stone
Related chakra: Sacral

Crystal meaning:

- Assists in severing old energy cords and attachments to previous sexual partners and experiences
- Activates fertility, new beginnings and rebirth
- Connects you to the energy of the divine masculine, invoking the energy of Shiva

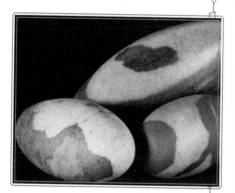

Smoky Quartz

Crystal colour: Smoky-coloured quartz
Related chakras: Base and sacral

Crystal meaning:

- Powerful grounding crystal
- Enhances a deep connection to Mother Earth and her healing vibration
- Facilitates your connection back to nature and allows you to receive the deep peace and tranquillity that comes with such an experience
- Transforms negative energy and thought forms, allowing you to feel rejuvenated

- Supports you in dissolving fears and limitations
- Assists you in moving through panic attacks and anxiety
- Reminds you to breathe deeply and embrace life

Sodalite

....

Crystal colour: Various shades of blue, white and black
Related chakras: Solar plexus and throat

Crystal meaning:

- Creates self-acceptance and enhances self-worth
- Deepens intuition
- Encourages you to believe in the divine essence of your soul
- Assists in healing your self-esteem and self-worth issues
- Enhances self-confidence
- Soothes, calms and heals the soul from any trauma

Spirit Quartz

Crystal colour: Range of lavender, pink and white
Related chakras: All

Crystal meaning:

- Opens you to your natural gifts and talents related to music and sound
- Enhances your creative musical passions and pursuits
- Opens you to the music of the cosmos
- Connects you to the fairy realm and nature spirits, creating a sense of magic in your life
- Balances the chakras and energy field, creating wellbeing

- Invokes inspiration and balance
- Aligns to the pure joy and freedom that is our divine birthright
- Connects you to the innocence and magic of the child within
- Unlocks and circulates stagnant energy

Stibnite

· · · · · · · · · · · · · ·

Crystal colour: Silver
Related chakra: Base, solar plexus and crown

Crystal meaning:

- Supports your personal empowerment and transformation
- Grounds your energy in the Earth so you feel supported
- Assists you in dealing with fear of conflict and confrontation
- Supports you to create healthy boundaries
- Supports those who suffer from chronic anxiety
- Enhances and supports the astral travel journey
- Assists in dissolving apprehension and uncertainty

Sugilite

Crystal colour: Various shades of purple, white and black
Related chakra: Heart

Crystal meaning:

- Allows you to live in the present moment where you can receive all the gifts life has to offer
- Strengthens your ability to walk your life path
- Enhances devotion to your divine path and purpose
- Enhances soul love and connection
  - Opens you to the divine truth and acceptance of your true mission on Earth

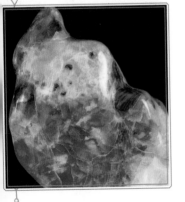

Shungite

Crystal colour: Black
Related chakra: Base

Crystal meaning:

- Allows you to deeply connect with your shadow side and receive the gifts it has to offer
- Brings balance
- Grounds and protects
- Supports deep self-reflection
- Assists in addressing and releasing painful, deep-seated negative behavioural patterns and cycles

Sunstone

Crystal colour: Various shades of creams and orange with tiny vibrant speckles

Related chakra: Solar plexus

Crystal meaning:

- Connects to the energy of the divine source of all things, invoking great personal power in your life
- Awakens self-empowerment, creating strength and courage
- Enhances leadership qualities and the ability to listen to your higher guidance

- Facilitates transformation
- Releases blockages and resistance to change
- Rekindles your passion for life
- Assists in bringing in the light of the soul, helping one to move through depression

Tanzanite

....

Crystal colour: Range of translucent to opaque purplish blues
Related chakra: Third eye

Crystal meaning:

- Opens you to your spiritual wisdom and sharing this knowledge from the heart
- Opens and activates the third eye chakra, enhancing clarity, vision and imagination
- Assists in communication with higher aspects of self, creating a deep knowing and wisdom in your life
- Supports you to make clear decisions in alignment with your soul purpose
- Allows you to see with clarity

Tektite

Crystal colour: Black
Related chakra: Crown

Crystal meaning:

- Enhances telepathic communication and intuitive gifts
- Connects you with light beings from other planets and dimensions to receive knowledge, support and positive direction in life
- Creates a strong protective energy shield around the aura
- Facilitates the connection to aspects of yourself in other dimensions and planes of existence

Tibetan Quartz

Crystal colour: Clear Quartz with black inclusions
Related chakras: All

Crystal meaning:

- Holds all the properties of Clear Quartz
- Resonates to the powerful energy of Tibet and its deep wisdom
- Allows you to find a place of peace and serenity

Tiger's Eye

Crystal colour: Varieties of browns, oranges, blacks and golds with reddish tinges

Related chakras: Sacral and solar plexus

Crystal meaning:

- Allows you to see clearly into situations, making it a powerful crystal to assist in decision making
- Allows you to open deeply to spiritual wisdom and live it on a day-to-day basis

- Enhances courage and strength in your life
- Allows you to stay focused on the task
- Supports us in challenging and confrontational situations
- Supports us in finding our inner truths and draws in the courage from our spirit to face our challenges

Topaz

. . . .

Crystal colour: Varied range of opaque to translucent colours, from clear to browns, greens, reds, whites, blues and yellows
Related chakras: All

Crystal meaning:

- Powerful crystal to assist in manifestation and aligning to your higher purpose
- Clears and cleanses the mind, creating clarity and a deeper sense of peace
- Opens the crown chakra, bringing in the light of the cosmos for purification
- Facilitates spiritual and creative expression
- Calms and soothes the heart
- Brings in a deeper gratitude and appreciation of our gifts

Tourmaline – Black

Crystal colour: Black
Related chakras: Base

Crystal meaning:

- Powerful grounding and protective crystal
- Transmutes and dissolves any stuck or dormant energies in the body and auric field, creating a deep and powerful cleansing and purification
- Strengthens and protects the aura, allowing you to feel safe in your own energy field

- Assists in creating appropriate boundaries in your life
- Powerful crystal to have around computers and telephones to dissolve unwanted electromagnetic energy
- Unblocks and circulates stagnant energy

Tourmaline – Dravite (Brown)

Crystal colour: Brown
Related chakra: Base and sacral

Crystal meaning:

- Assists in healing past sexual issues, allowing you to move into a loving sexual union with your beloved
- Activates and stimulates the base and sacral chakras, and assists in healing issues related to these chakras
- Creates stability and grounding in your life, allowing you to feel safe and supported
- Allows you to release any fear of change and move forward
- Assists in releasing suppressed anger, frustration, sadness and disappointment

Tourmaline – Green

Crystal colour: Opaque to translucent green
Related chakra: Heart

Crystal meaning:

- Deep connection to the Earth and nature spirits
- Opens you to receive the healing energy and wisdom held deep within the Earth
- Purifies and strengthens the nervous system
- Balances and harmonises the heart chakra, allowing for healing around any old wounds of the heart
- Creates forgiveness and understanding
- Sets you free from the restraints of fear
- Encourages honouring of self and others

Tourmaline – Indicolite (Blue)

Crystal colour: Opaque to translucent blue
Related chakras: Throat and third eye

Crystal meaning:

- Deepens your intuition and psychic gifts
- Assists in the communication and expression of true self from a deeper level of truth
- Balances the mind and heart, allowing for a deeper space of inner peace
- Allows you to move through shyness and more into your true essence

Tourmaline – Pink

Crystal colour: Opaque to translucent pinks
Related chakras: Heart

Crystal meaning:

- Stone of grace, aligning your soul to this sacred and divine vibration
- Assists in releasing blame and guilt, allowing you to find a place of deep forgiveness
- Powerfully opens and heals the heart, allowing you to come from a deeper place of unconditional love
- Transforms any barriers or walls around the heart chakra, allowing you to be open to the flow of giving and receiving
- Opens you to experience the magic and joy that life has to share with us

Tourmaline – Rubellite (Red)

Crystal colour: Opaque to translucent red
Related chakra: Sacral

Crystal meaning:

- Enhances passion, strength and vitality
- Awakens your inspiration and positive outlook and zest for life
- Opens you to your passion and creativity
- Good for teachers to keep the vibe and energy high in the room
- Reignites the eternal flame within
- Rejuvenates and restores energy
- Revitalises the spirit
- Releases worry and negative thinking

Tourmaline – Watermelon

Crystal colour: Pink and green
Related chakras: Heart

Crystal meaning:

- Stone of humility, aligning your soul to this powerful and divine vibration
- Amplifies qualities of Green and Pink Tourmaline; the synergy of the pink and green crystals brings a powerful balancing and healing of the heart chakra, allowing you to love unconditionally
- Opens and encourages you to experience the joy of life
- Amplifies forgiveness and compassion on a global scale

Tree Root (Petrified)

Crystal colour: Creams to dark browns
Related chakra: Base

Crystal meaning:

- Deepens connection to our ancestors and their deep wisdom
- Allows you to have your feet planted on the ground, creating balance and stability
- Grounds and supports
- Deepens connection to the ancient tree beings on the Earth and their healing energy

Turquoise

Crystal colour: Turquoise
Related chakras: Heart and throat

Crystal meaning:

- Encourages you to listen from the heart
- Deepens clarity and knowing of your true feelings and how to express them from a place of love
- Opens you to feel, experience and express your own truth
- Promotes honesty and integrity in your life
- Opens the heart, allowing you to speak from a deep place of clarity and truth
- Enhances self-expression

Vivianite

....

Crystal colour: Dark green and blue
Related chakras: Heart and throat

Crystal meaning:

- Powerfully transforms issues of the heart, allowing you to flow free in the essence of love
- Awakens deep inspiration and success in your life
- Connects to the joy and wonder of life

Zincite

Crystal colour: Variety of orange, yellow and green
Related chakras: All

Crystal meaning:

- Strengthens the bonds of family, tribe and community
- Stimulates your creative flow
- Deepens connection with the infinite possibilities of your life

ABOUT RACHELLE

Rachelle Charman is the founder and principal of The Academy of Crystal Awakening. She spends her free time in union and ceremony with sacred land, honouring Mother Earth and sharing in her ancient wisdom. Rachelle receives her teachings directly from her own life experiences, the Crystal Kingdom and Mother Earth herself as she truly embodies and radiates her deep wisdom. In her powerful connection to the Crystal Kingdom and understanding of the healing gifts and tools of the Earth, Rachelle has received profound healing and experienced a deep awakening of the self.

Rachelle's teachings are truly dynamic, heartfelt and life changing. In her deep passion for assisting humanity in embracing self-love and acceptance, Rachelle offers her fellow students her advanced knowledge in the healing gifts offered by the Crystal Kingdom, those special gems and stones that can only be considered as a gift from Heaven to Earth.

By taking a step into your heart and learning the healing powers and processes offered by Rachelle, the Crystal Kingdom and Mother Earth, you will open up to a world of self-healing where unconditional love fills every cell of your being. Crystals embody not only simplistic beauty, but a multitude of energies that activate our mind, body and soul. Rachelle certainly embodies their gifts and knowledge.

Rachelle's teachings flow naturally from the heart and are strongly driven by her love of humanity. She embodies and lives her divine mission for sharing her love of and passion for the Earth's medicines. She is recognised globally for her depth and authenticity. Rachelle is a dynamic and passionate teacher, and travels the world with her teachings, paving the way for others to reconnect to their own innate shamanic wisdom and realign to the organic flow of Mother Earth's love, healing and wisdom. She is well known throughout the world for her organic, loving, down-to-earth personality and truly radiates Divine Love.

For more information please visit www.crystalawakening.com